YOUR KNOWLEDGE HAS VALUE

Anastasia Castillo

Folk Etymology as a Linguistic Phenomenon

GRIN Publishing

Bibliographic information published by the German National Library:

The German National Library lists this publication in the National Bibliography; detailed bibliographic data are available on the Internet at http://dnb.dnb.de .

Imprint:

Copyright © 2007 GRIN Verlag, Open Publishing GmbH
Print and binding: Books on Demand GmbH, Norderstedt Germany
ISBN: 978-3-640-70590-0

This book at GRIN:

http://www.grin.com/en/e-book/156567/folk-etymology-as-a-linguistic-phenomenon

GRIN - Your knowledge has value

Since its foundation in 1998, GRIN has specialized in publishing academic texts by students, college teachers and other academics as e-book and printed book. The website www.grin.com is an ideal platform for presenting term papers, final papers, scientific essays, dissertations and specialist books.

Visit us on the internet:

http://www.grin.com/

http://www.facebook.com/grincom

http://www.twitter.com/grin_com

Westfälische Wilhelms – Universität Münster

Englisches Seminar
Hauptseminar „English Semantics"
WS 2007/2008

Ausarbeitung zum Thema:

Folk Etymology as a Linguistic Phenomenon

Table of contents

Introduction

"Words are not only the elements of a language, but also of the history of the people speaking it. They are important milestones along the way leading to the majestic Palace of Human Knowledge."[1]

E. Klein

The English language belongs to the Indo-European group of languages. Modern English is regarded as the global lingua franca. The language is widely spoken all over the world and we encounter it in business, science, technology, advertising, travel, and some other domains. However, how could the language originally spoken by a few thousand Anglo-Saxons establish such dominance? The language evolved over centuries and how much the language has change since then is all too clear. Some of the words in present day English date back to Old English, while others come from many of the Indo-European languages. The arrival of other cultures to England had a significant impact on English linguistic history. The influence of Scandinavian, Latin and Romance languages can be clearly seen at all linguistic levels in English language.

Historical linguistics is the study of language change. One of its main concerns is the study of the history of words. The discipline that analyses the origin, formation, and development of the word is defined as etymology. It is also a combination of word analysis and the study of literary text across language and time. However, it would not have developed into such an interesting discipline without the linguistic phenomenon of folk etymology. A foreign word that was hard to pronounce would be changed into something that sounded more familiar. Sometimes the change was made unconsciously due to mishearing or misunderstanding. This process frequently occurs when one language borrows a word from another. Since the Norman Conquest the English language was constantly adopting words due to external cultural influences. It is not entirely clear how many words entered English from other languages. But the meaning of some of them has also certainly changed. According to D. Crystal "most of the words in the language have changed their meaning over the past thousand years, their original meanings forgotten".[2] Nevertheless, at that stage of development it is still possible for

---

[1] Ernest Klein, "Introduction". In *A comprehensive etymological dictionary of the English language.* (Amsterdam, London, New York, 1966), 10.
[2] David Crystal, *The stories of English* (London, 2005).

etymology to identify whether the change in a word or phrase's meaning was made due to cultural influence or whether it is a case of folk etymology.

The evolution of English language can not be considered separately from the country's history. Therefore the first chapter of this essay outlines some of the historical background to the English language, presented chronologically from Old English to Modern English. The second chapter is devoted to the term *etymology*, distinguishing this term from *folk etymology* by giving definitions for both terms and providing some examples of folk etymology. The final chapter provides answers for task 4.3.3.1 from *Natural Language Semantics* by Keith Allan. The essay ends with a conclusion.

Chapter 1. Historical development of the English language

Old English

The history of the English language started with the arrival of Germanic tribes, the Angles, the Saxons and the Jutes, who invaded Britain during the 5th century AD. They came from the European mainland, what is today Denmark and northern Germany, and displaced the multilingual British population. Britain at this time was full of people with different ethnic backgrounds – Britons themselves (also called Celts), the Scots, the Picts, and the Romans, who ruled there until the early 5th century. According to D. Crystal "Old English, […], evolved in a land which was full of migrants, raiders, mercenaries, temporary settlers, long-established families, people of mixed ethnic origins, and rapidly changing power bases."[1] So due to the varied origins of the British inhabitants Old English consisted of the diverse group of dialects. Eventually, a single language, also called Anglo-Saxon, was established. The new settlers formed kingdoms and sub-kingdoms and by the 9th century Britain was divided into four kingdoms - Northumbria, Mercia, East Anglia and Wessex with consequently four major dialect areas. Around the 10th century one of these dialects, West Saxon, came to dominate. It also was a language of literature and political power in the land. It is significant for that period that the first sings of language standardisation were made. The surviving manuscripts display for example a lesser dialect mixture and remarkable similarity in spelling and word construction.

The Anglo-Saxon period lasted for 600 years, from 410 to 1066, and during that time the Old English underwent many changes. First of all, it was influenced by Celtic-speaking inhabitants from Scotland, Ireland, Cornwall and Wales. There are large numbers of Celtic place-names in England that were simply taken over by Anglo-Saxons, i.e. Avon or Leeds, as well as numerous compound names. The meaning most of them has to do with features of the landscape, such as *cumb* or *comb* (valley) in *Cambridge*, *dun* (hill) in *Doncaster*, *lin* (lake) in *Lincoln*, *bre* or *pen* for "hill" in *Penrith*.[2] Although the presence of Celtic place-names is still obvious in nowadays England, the etymology of many domestic words that are considered to be of Celtic origin is doubtful since it is hard to prove whether the word entered the Old English from Celtic language or from Latin. The chief difficulty lies in the fact that the Celts

---

[1] David Crystal, *The stories of English* (London, 2005).
[2] Cf. ibid., http://www.askoxford.com/worldofwords/history/?view=uk.

were familiar with Latin due to the Roman occupation. Thus, Latin could to some degree have had an influence on early Celtic. The process of borrowing from Latin continued throughout the Old English period. With the growth of Church's influence a large number of religious words and words of educated character entered the language mostly through written manuscripts. A selection of words borrowed from Latin is given in the following panel.

Some words borrowed from Latin c. 450 – 1100

Old English	Modern English	Latin origin
lǽden	Latin	ladinus
mǽgester	master	magister
relic	relic	reliquia
segn	mark, sign	signum
alter	altar	altar
fers	verse	versus
orgel	organ	organum
scol	school	scola

Source: David Crystal, *The stories of English* (London, 2005, 62, 64)

On the Vikings' arrival to England in the late 8th century many Scandinavian loanwords were introduced into the language. The Danes and Northmen came over to England in great numbers providing new words, culture, and a new political power. Some of them survived into modern Standard English (i.e. *dream* derived from Scandinavian *draumr,* meaning "joy", or *shirt* formed from *skirt*).[1] Some new place-names with Scandinavian origin also enriched English place-name history.

Middle English

The influence of French upon English language is well known. The major impact took place after the Norman Conquest in 1066. It did not happen overnight though, for loanwords to become established. The merchants from the European mainland and English traders themselves had already brought some French words during the Anglo-Saxon period. For England being under the Norman French rule in the 11th and 12th centuries French became a language of government and law, whereas English continued to be the language of common people. Latin by this time was accepted as the language of law, literature, and the church. Thus, in the early Middle

---

[1] Cf. http://www.anglik.net/englishlanguagehistory.htm.

Ages, Anglo-Norman England was a trilingual nation. But it was not to last long. English was eventually reasserted as the main official language, French ceased to be used, and Latin maintained to be the medium of education and the church. From a linguistic point of view, some remarkable changes were made in the language. The vocabulary grew enormously, a series of changes in pronunciation also occurred in English, and some grammatical transformation such as word order and prepositional constructions took place at this period.

There are some other sources of foreign words in Old and Middle English. There is a proven evidence that a very few words were borrowed from Old Slavic language, such as the words *taper-œxe* or *sable*. The word *taper-œxe* entered Middle English from Old Norse which in turn got it from Old Slavic. Modern Russian still has it as топор [*topor*], meaning 'axe'[1]. Such languages as German, and Sanskrit also affected English. On the other hand, a considerable number of German words were borrowed indirectly, through the French language. A large number of words came from the Middle East – from Arabic, such as *zenith, amber, syrup, hazard*, or from Persian (*chess, rook, checkmate*).

Early Modern English

In the late medieval and early modern period the literary language began to evolve, culminating in the works of Geoffrey Chaucer whose significant use of different dialects in his *The Canterbury Tales* made this composition even more interesting for historical linguists. Linguistic discussions in Old and Middle English focused rather on Latin grammar, the nature of translation, and the differences in style. In England, at the end of the Middle Ages, a standard language began to emerge. It underwent major changes in pronunciation (i.e. the Great Vowel Shift)[2], its lexicon was continued to grow rapidly due to large numbers of loanwords especially during the Renaissance when classical scholarships brought many Latin and Greek words into the language. People began to distinguish between written and spoken English. It was already an official language of the court and the Parliament, and with introduction of the printing press by William Caxton in 1476 books started to be seen as commodities with the result of the reduced numbers of illiterate people. Just a century later significant levels of standardization were found in printed books. The standard was the London dialect,

---

[1] David Crystal, *The stories of English* (London, 2005).
[2] Cf. http://www.askoxford.com/worldofwords/history/?view=uk.

where the most books were published. The crucial event also occurred in the history of Church. English was by this time beginning to be used in services and some first Bibles were printed in English. At the turn of the 17th century the English alphabet was fixed consisting of 26 letters. Interest in word etymology grew and the first dictionaries of English language were produced at the same time.

Late Modern English

There are two main historical factors that played an important role in evolution of the Late Modern English. The first factor was the industrial revolution in the 19th century. It had a great impact on vocabulary since the technological progress brought many new words referring to science and technology, though mainly of Latin or Creek origin. The second factor was the rise of the British Empire and the growth of colonization and overseas trade. The result was a global spread of the English language.

However, not only English was introduced to the world. Many other languages made their contribution into expansion of English language. Its dialects developed in the former colonies of the British Empire. Now it is a good example of a pluricentric language[1]. Therefore, the linguistic changes will appear in the language as long as it stays in the process of development.

---

[1] Cf. David Crystal, *The stories of English* (London, 2005).

Chapter 2. Definition of *etymology* and *folk etymology*

As mentioned in the introduction, etymology is the study of the history of words. The term is derived from the Greek words ἔτυμον *(etymon)*, denoting 'true meaning', and λόγος *(lógos)*, meaning 'word'. Etymology was already known in antiquity when a progressive achievement was made – the discovery that "certain words, perhaps the majority of lexemes, have the built-in capacity to migrate from one locus, or one speech community, to another – as part of the general cultural heritage."[1] The ancient philosophers considered "the recovering the original names [...] as equivalent to recovering the truth of the things"[2], *nomen est omen*. However, by etymologizing a name they provided no scientific explanation of it in the modern sense. In early Greece etymology was regarded as a technique of rhetoric and philosophy. In Plato's dialogue *Cratylus* (with its subtitle *On the propriety of names*), one of the first works on the theory of the relation between words and things, he tried to explain that "language is entirely conventional in its signification by producing a variety of etymological accounts of the meanings of words"[3]. At the same time etymology tended to become a part of grammatical explanation.

The approach to etymology in medieval Europe was in a sort of juxtaposition or inventory. Rather than a stable discipline with fixed procedures and theories, etymology was a form of wordplay, in which the origins of the words were often guessed. However, it has to be emphasized that the primary attempts to write an etymological dictionary were made at this time, and yet most of these dictionaries lacked evidence and credibility.

The real interest in word etymology as a scientific discipline grew around the 16th century when this scholarship started to develop in several advanced European countries. Etymological arguments of speculative character were left behind, while attention was paid to historical facts focusing on the place and time of a word's beginning, its earliest signification and syntactic construction. The number of etymological methods increased during this time and beside the great attention was paid to the vast diversity of language' dialects. Now it is a well-known fact that in the course of the last few centuries, etymology has reached a high degree of development.

---

[1] Yakov Malkiel, *Etymology* (Cambridge, 1993).
[2] Mark Amsler, *Etymology and grammatical discourse in late antiquity and the early middle ages* (Amsterdam/ Philadelphia, 1989).
[3] Ibid.; cf. Keith Allan, *Natural Language Semantics* (Oxford, 2001).

There are several types of etymological explanations:

- translating or interpreting the meaning of a loan word or foreign word[1] (interpretatio);
- dividing a word into its components and explaining its origins (compositio);
- word formation such as derivation (derivatio);
- associating one word with another on the basis of either sound similarity or a connection between meanings (expositio).[2]

Another two important aspects of etymological theory should also be mentioned: the origin of words tends to become more confusing over time due to sound change and semantic change. Sound change refers to a process of language change that affects pronunciation. It can be illustrated, for example, by the change in the pronunciation of words containing *sk* from /sk/ to /ʃ/ by Anglo-Saxons, such as Latin *scrinium*, meaning 'a chest for books and papers' (pronounced with /sk-/) and Old English *scrin* (pronounced with /ʃ-/).[3] Semantic change deals with meaning, when a new meaning of a word is added to already existing meaning(s), for example a new meaning of the word *mouse* referring to computer language.

The vocabulary of English, which was influenced by so many other languages as is shown in the preceding chapter, contains many words of uncertain or unknown etymology. A popular but mistaken account of the origin of a word or phrase is called folk etymology.

The term *folk etymology* was firstly introduced in 1852 in an article "German Folk Etymology" by Ernst Förstemann (1822 - 1906), German librarian and historian. Förstemann is also ranked as a founder of onomatology, the study of proper names of all kinds and their origins. Folk etymology can be defined as a process of consciously or unconsciously changing the shape of a word to reproduce the existing morphemes in a language. Generally, this process requires some changes in pronunciation and / or spelling. Thus, only if a word has changed from its original form that was borrowed from other language and the meaning of the original word was reinterpreted, can the term be referred to as folk etymology.

---

[1] Loan words become a virtual native and can hardly be identified, for example *bishop* and *street*, whereas foreign words are partially assimilated and are harder to be recognized as borrowings, like *hotel* (from Fr. hôtel).
[2] Cf. Mark Amsler, *Etymology and grammatical discourse in late antiquity and the early middle ages* (Amsterdam, Philadelphia, 1989).
[3] Cf. David Crystal, *The stories of English* (London, 2005).

Generally, there are two main classes of folk etymology, depending on whether a formal relationship was involved in word evolution and word formation, or, if at the same time the word meaning and logical connection were influenced. Word development that has substantially changed in meaning is of most interest since they are considered to be totally new words in the language.[1] The transformation the words undergo in order to resemble other words is often seen in the case of unusual words, such as the names of flowers, diseases, or medicines.

The following examples show some of the famous folk etymologies:

• *bridegroom:* this word derives from Old English *brȳdguma, brȳd,* meaning 'bride', and *guma,* meaning 'man' (Old Saxon *brūdigomo,* Dutch *bruidegom,* Old Hoch German *brūtigomo).* A bride's man is a corruption from a confusion of *gome* (Gothic *guma,* Latin *homo*) with *grome,* a groom or a servant from Old French *gromme.*

• *penthouse:* one of the meanings in Modern English is an apartment or suite on the top floor of a tall building, especially as associated with being expensive or luxurious. The word was first originated in 1520-1530 from Middle English *pentis* (rarely *pendis*), entering through Anglo-Norman from Old French *apentis,* meaning 'to hang against' that was derived from late Latin medicine term *appendicium* from the verb *appendere,* meaning 'hang on, attach in a dependent state'.

• *sand-blind:* means 'half-blind, purblind'. The Old English word *samblind* was replaced by *sand-blind* when the element *sam* lost its meaning as 'half' which was a short form of West German *sami-* (represented by Old Saxon *sām-* or Old High German *sāmi-*). A quotation in the *Folk-Etymology* gives a line of Shakespeare's *The Merchant of Venice:* "More than *sand-blind,* high gravel blind" (ii, 2).[2]

Intentional perversion of words that we can meet in works of fiction is to be distinguished from true folk etymologies. The author's main purpose is to raise a laugh at illiterate personages, such as Mrs. Bennett in *Pride and Prejudice* or Myrtle Wilson in *The great Gatsby.*

However erroneous the folk etymologies may be, many of the words created in this way have become standard through long-term use.

---

[1] Cf. Karl Gustav Andersen, *Deutsche Volksetymologie* (Leipzig, 1919).
[2] Folk-Etymology. A dictionary of verbal corruptions or words perverted in form or meaning, by false derivation or mistaken analogy. (New York, 1969).

Chapter 3. Task solution

In this chapter an attempt is made to give the solution for the task 4.3.3.1. The task consists of three parts that listed as a), b), and c). The original form of the words given has to be found followed by explanation of the process that probably happened. *The Oxford dictionary of English etymology* and *the Oxford English Dictionary online* are the main sources to solve the task given.

a). The words given are: *apron, adder, orange, nickname,* and *pea.*

apron evolved by misdivision of Middle English *a napron* as *an apron* in the 14th century. The Latin word *mappa* (napkin) was replaced by Old French *naperon*, meaning 'table-cloth' that was in turn undertaken by Middle English.

adder entered the language from Old English *næd(d)re*, meaning 'snake', and is related to Latin *natrix* (water-snake). As in the example above, original *n* has been lost by coalescence with a preceding indefinite article. Thus, *a nadder* became *an adder* around 14th century. It is remarkable that the word corresponding to *næd(d)re* existed in other languages, too - for example, in Old Saxon it was *nādra*, in Middle Dutch *nadre*, in Old High German *nātara*, and in Old Norse *naðr(a)*.

orange arrived in English in the 14th century from Old French *orenge* in *pomme d'orenge*, corresponding to Spanish *naranja*, Portuguese *laranja*, Italian *narancia*. The fruit came presumably from India and was introduced in Italy in the 11th century. The word for orange in late Sanskrit was *nāranga*, in Arabic *nāranj*, and in Persian *nārang*. Likewise the previous examples show, loss of initial *n* was probably due to the confusion with indefinite article. Since the 16th century the word is also used as the name of a colour.

nickname is in use since the late Middle English period, into which it had been taken from Old Norse *aukanafn*. Middle English *nekename* was a misdivision of *ekename* and *eke* was a variation of Old English *ecan*, meaning 'addition' or 'an increase'.

pea evolved as false singular from Middle English *pease* (plural – *pesen*, meaning 'weight'), but was mistaken for a plural of Old French *peis*. The dish *pea porridge* dates to the 16th century and *pea soup* is first recoded two centuries later in 1711. At the end of the century the dish is recoded as the children's rhyme:

peas porridge hot,

peas porridge cold,

peas porridge in the pot nine days old.[1]

b). The next phrase is *I could **of** done it.*

One of the principal distinguishes between standard and non-standard English is grammatical variation. There are some grammatical features in the noun phrase (i.e. *hisself* instead of *himself*), in the verb phrase (i.e. *in't* instead of *is not*), and in a clause that are usually identified as non-standard English. In the phrase *I could **of** done it* preposition *of* is used for auxiliary verb 'have' that according to the *OED online* is arisen through misapprehension of the verb. This usage was believed to appear in 20th century. In fact it entered the language much earlier as seen in John Keats' letter dated 1819 where he wrote *I should not **of** written.*[2]

c). The words given are: the distress call *Mayday*, the score *love* in tennis, the phrase *check mate* in chess, and the compound noun *chaise-lounge*.

Mayday is used as an international radio distress signal especially by ships and aircraft. The word corresponds to the French pronunciation of the expression *m'aider*, meaning 'come help me!'.

The score ***love*** in games including tennis has been used since the 18th century in the sense of 'no score'. It derives from the phrase *playing for love,* meaning to play for nothing, without any stakes and is first recorded in the 17th century.

Check mate is a move in chess that means that a chess-player to whom checkmate has been given is defeated. The first quotation in the *OED online* refers to the late 14th century. The word entered English language from Persian *shah mat*, meaning 'the king is dead' that was later replaced by Old French *eschec mat*.

Chaise-lounge was corrupted in the 19th century from French *chaise longue*, meaning 'long chair'. The misspelling of *chaise longue* was due to a conflation of French *longue* (long) with English *lounge*.

---

[1] David Wilton, *World myths. Debunking linguistics urban legends* (Oxford, 2004).
[2] Cf. David Crystal, *The stories of English* (London, 2005).

Conclusion

"Language is a mirror in which the whole spiritual development of mankind reflects itself"[1]. Consequently, the social changes experienced by a nation are likewise reflected in its language. English, since its very beginning as an Anglo-Saxon dialect in multilingual Britain up to its position as a global language today, has undergone considerable linguistic development. This linguistic evolution was mainly caused by frequent political regime changes, which brought with them the influence of other languages. Scandinavian languages shaped English during the Anglo-Saxon period, producing a range of dialects. The Norman Conquest of 1066 brought many French words into English. Greek and Latin words began to enter in the 15th century. Later on the invention of the printing press allowed the standard language to spread more rapidly and widely. Modern English dating from 1500 continued to borrow words from other languages and has coined many new words to reflect advances in technology and science.

Since there are many words from different languages in English, etymologists have spent much time investigating the origin of these words. However, because of the high presence of loan and foreign words in English, the risk of mispronunciation or misspelling was high. This resulted in such linguistic phenomenon as folk etymology, a particularly interesting way of researching a language's development.

---

[1] Ernest Klein, "Introduction". In *A comprehensive etymological dictionary of the English language.* (Amsterdam, London, New York, 1966), 10.

Bibliography:

1. *A comprehensive etymological dictionary of the English language*. Ed. E. Klein. Amsterdam, London, New York, 1966.

2. Allan, Keith. *Natural Language Semantics.* Oxford, 2001

3. Amsler, Mark. *Etymology and grammatical discourse in late antiquity and the early middle ages.* Amsterdam, Philadelphia, 1989.

4. Andersen, Karl Gustav. *Deutsche Volksetymologie*. Leipzig, 1919.

5. Crystal, David. *The stories of English*. London, 2005.

6. *Folk-Etymology. A dictionary of verbal corruptions or words perverted in form or meaning, by false derivation or mistaken analogy.* Ed. Rev. A. Smythe Palmer. New York, 1969.

7. Malkiel, Yakov. *Etymology.* Cambridge, 1993.

8. *The Oxford dictionary of English etymology*. Ed. C. T. Onions. Oxford, 1966.

9. Wilton, David. *World myths. Debunking linguistics urban legends*. Oxford, 2004.

10. Durkin, Philip. "History of English. Five events that shaped the history of English".
    http://www.askoxford.com/worldofwords/history/?view=uk (Abruf: 15.01.2008)

11. "The history of the English Language – an introduction".
    http://www.anglik.net/englishlanguagehistory.htm (Abruf: 17.01.2008)